JUDITH BAKER MONTANO'S

Embroidery & Crazy Quilt
STITCH TOOL

- 180+ STITCHES & COMBINATIONS
- TIPS FOR NEEDLES, THREAD, RIBBON, FABRIC
- ILLUSTRATIONS FOR LEFT-HANDED & RIGHT-HANDED ST

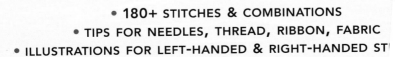

Text copyright © 2008 by Judith Baker Montano

Artwork copyright © 2008 by C&T Publishing, Inc.

Publisher: Amy Marson

Editorial Director: Gailen Runge

Acquisitions Editor: Jan Grigsby

Editor: Liz Aneloski

Technical Editor: Teresa Stroin

Copyeditor: Stacy Chamness

Proofreader: Wordfirm Inc.

Cover Designer/Designer: Kristen Yenche

Production Coordinator: Kirstie L. Pettersen

Illustrator: Kirstie L. Pettersen and Richard Sheppard

Photography by Christina-Carty Francis and Diane Pedersen of C&T Publishing unless otherwise noted.

Published by C&T Publishing, Inc., P.O. Box 1456, Lafayette, CA 94549

Attention Teachers: C&T Publishing, Inc., encourages you to use this book as a text for teaching. Contact us at 800-284-1114 or www.ctpub.com for more information about the C&T Teachers' Program.

We take great care to ensure that the information included in our products is accurate and presented in good faith, but no warranty is provided nor are results guaranteed. Having no control over the choices of materials or procedures used, neither the author nor C&T Publishing, Inc., shall have any liability to any person or entity with respect to any loss or damage caused directly or indirectly by the information contained in this book. For your convenience, we post an up-to-date listing of corrections on our website (www.ctpub.com). If a correction is not already noted, please contact our customer service department at ctinfo@ctpub.com or at P.O. Box 1456, Lafayette, CA 94549.

Trademark (™) and registered trademark (®) names are used throughout this book. Rather than use the symbols with every occurrence of a trademark or registered trademark name, we are using the names only in the editorial fashion and to the benefit of the owner, with no intention of infringement.

Printed in China

10

Contents

Stitch Index

ALGERIAN EYE STITCH
23

ARROWHEAD STITCH
24

ARROWHEAD STITCH (STACKED)
25

BACKSTITCH
26

BACKSTITCH (STAR STITCH)
27

BACKSTITCH (THREADED)
28

BASQUE STITCH
29

BOSNIAN STITCH
30

BRADFORD ROSE
31

BRAID STITCH
32

BULLION ROSE
33

BULLION ROSEBUD
34

BULLION STITCH
35

BUTTONHOLE STITCH
36

BUTTONHOLE STITCH (CIRCLE)
37

BUTTONHOLE STITCH (CLOSED)
38

BUTTONHOLE STITCH (DETACHED)
39

BUTTONHOLE STITCH (KNOTTED)
40

BUTTONHOLE STITCH (TRIANGLE)
41

BUTTONHOLE STITCH (UP AND DOWN)
42

CABLE STITCH
43

CAST-ON STITCH FLOWER
44

CHAIN ROSE
45

CHAIN STITCH
46

CHAIN STITCH
(CABLE)
47

CHAIN STITCH
(CROCHET)
48

CHAIN STITCH
(DETACHED TWISTED)
49

CHAIN STITCH
(FLOWER;
DETACHED)
50

CHAIN STITCH
(MAGIC)
51

CHAIN STITCH
(OPEN)
52

CHAIN STITCH
(ROSETTE)
53

CHAIN STITCH
(RUSSIAN)
54

CHAIN STITCH
(SPINY)
55

CHAIN STITCH
(TWISTED)
56

CHAIN STITCH
(WHIPPED)
57

CHAIN STITCH
(ZIGZAG)
58

CHEVRON STITCH
59

CHINESE KNOT
(LOOPED)
61

CHINESE KNOT
(PEKING KNOT)
60

CHRISTINE'S
BLOSSOM
62

COLONIAL KNOT
63

CONCERTINA ROSE
64

CORAL STITCH
65

CORAL STITCH
(ZIGZAG)
66

COUCHED ROSE
67

COUCHING STITCH
68

CRETAN STITCH
69

CRETAN STITCH
(DECORATIVE)
70

CROSS STITCH
71

CROSS STITCH
(FLOWER)
72

CROSS STITCH
(ST. GEORGE)
73

CROWN STITCH
74

DOUBLE KNOT
75

ELLY'S
WIRE-RIBBON PANSY
76

ERMINE STITCH
77

EYELET FLOWER
78

EYELETS (FREEFORM)
79

FEATHER STITCH
80

FEATHER STITCH
(CHAINED)
81

FEATHER STITCH
(CLOSED)
82

FEATHER STITCH
(LEAF)
83

FERN LEAF STITCH
84

FISHBONE STITCH
85

FIVE-PETAL
GATHERED FLOWER
86

FLAT STITCH
87

FLY STITCH
88

FLY STITCH (CIRCLE)
89

FLY STITCH
(DANDELION
SEED POD)
90

FLY STITCH (LEAF)
91

FOLDED ROSEBUD
92

FREEFORM FLOWER
93

FRENCH KNOT
94

FRENCH KNOT
FLOWER
95

FRENCH KNOT
LOOP STITCH
96

GATHERED RIBBON
FLOWER
97

GRANITO
98

HEAD OF THE
BULL STITCH
99

HELEN'S ANTIQUE ROSE
100

HERRINGBONE STITCH
101

HERRINGBONE STITCH (LACED)
102

HOLBEIN STITCH
103

IRIS STITCH
104

JAN'S ANTIQUE ROSE
105

JAPANESE RIBBON STITCH
106

JAPANESE WIRE RIBBON BUD
107

JOYCE FLOWER (FARGO FLOWER)
108

JUDITH'S CURLED LEAF
109

JUDITH'S KNOTTED FLOWERS
110

LAZY DAISY STITCH
111

LAZY DAISY STITCH (BULLION KNOT)
112

LAZY DAISY STITCH (BULLION TIP)
113

LAZY DAISY STITCH (DECORATIVE)
114

LAZY DAISY STITCH (DOUBLE)
115

LAZY DAISY STITCH (FRENCH KNOT)
116

LAZY DAISY STITCH ROSE
117

LAZY DAISY STITCH (ROSEBUD)
118

LEAF RIBBON STITCH
119

LEAF STITCH
120

LEAVES (RIBBON)
121

LONG AND SHORT STITCH
122

LOOP FLOWER
123

LOOP FLOWER (BUD)
124

LOOP STITCH (SINGLE)
125

LOOP STITCH
(THREAD)
126

MAGIC CHAIN
BAND STITCH
127

MAIDENHAIR STITCH
128

MOKUBA FLOWER
129

MONTANO KNOT
130

NEEDLEWEAVING
BAR STITCH
131

NET STITCH
132

OPEN SQUARE
STITCH
133

OVERCAST STITCH
134

OYSTER STITCH
135

PALESTRINA KNOT
136

PALESTRINA KNOT
(SQUARED)
137

PANSY STITCH
138

PEKINESE STITCH
139

PISTIL STITCH
140

PLUME STITCH
141

PORTUGUESE
KNOTTED STEM
142

RAISED RIBBON
STITCH
143

RAISED STRAIGHT
STITCH
144

RAMBLER ROSE
145

RIBBON SPLIT STITCH
146

RIBBON STITCH
PANSY
147

ROSETTE BUD
148

ROSETTE STITCH
149

RUNNING STITCH
150

RUNNING STITCH
(LACED/WHIPPED)
151

RUTH'S ROSETTE
152

SATIN STITCH
153

SCROLL STITCH
154

SEED STITCH
155

SHEAF STITCH
156

SIDE RIBBON STITCH
157

SNAIL TRAIL STITCH
158

SPIDER WEB
(BACKSTITCH)
159

SPIDER WEB (ROSE)
160

SPLIT STITCH
161

STAB STITCH
162

STAR FILLING STITCH
163

STEM STITCH
164

STEM STITCH
(PORTUGUESE)
165

STEM STITCH
(WHIPPED)
166

STRAIGHT STITCH
167

STRAIGHT STITCH
(BUD)
168

STRAIGHT STITCH
(ROSE)
169

STRING OF
PEARLS STITCH
170

TUBE ROSE
171

TULIP STITCH
172

TURKEY-WORK
STITCH
173

TWISTED LOOP
STITCH
174

TWISTED RIBBON
STITCH
175

VAN DYKE STITCH
176

WHEAT EAR STITCH
177

WHEAT EAR STITCH
(DETACHED)
178

WHIP STITCH
(SINGLE & CURVED)
179

WOOL ROSE
180

WOOL ROSEBUD
181

WOVEN PICOT
STITCH
182

Getting Started

I hope you enjoy this easy-to-use *Embroidery & Crazy Quilt Stitch Tool*. We have included the stitches and some of the basic information from my best-selling books Elegant Stitches and Floral Stitches to get you started. The alphabetized stitches are offered with both right and left-handed diagrams in a handy stand up format. The small compact size is perfect for quick, take-along, reference.

Background Fabric Always add an extra 2″ to the fabric measurement to aid handling and stretching the fabric in a hoop or frame prior to stitching.

Ask yourself these questions when choosing a fabric:

1. Is the fabric appropriate for the subject matter?

2. How much wear and tear will the fabric receive?

3. Will the threads, yarns, or ribbons work up properly on the fabric selected?

- Plush, Velvet, and Wool—Use a large-eyed needle and stitches that will sit up on these fabrics so they don't get lost in the texture.

- Cotton, Polyester, Linen, and Shantung— These fabrics can support many types of embroidery.

- Moiré, Taffeta, Shot Cloth, and Satin—These fabrics take on an old-fashioned Victorian look that's good for fancywork associated with weddings or formal accessories.

- Lightweight Silk, Organza, and Batiste—These fabrics are very delicate and may need a bottom layer to stabilize them. Keep the thread and ribbon ends well concealed, or they may show through.

- Knits, Loosely Woven Fabric—Some of the loose weaves may need a stable fabric on the back to hold the stitches in place.

- Leather and Ultrasuede—Every hole must be punched with a stiletto.

Needles Be sure to use the proper needle; it will make your work much easier. The higher the number, the smaller the size and finer the needle.

- Beading—A very fine needle with a tiny eye strictly used for beading. Traditionally, they are quite long. There are also shorter sharps beading needles, excellent for picking up one bead at a time; I recommend a sharps #10.

- Betweens—A short needle with a small, round eye. Use for quilting and fine hand sewing.

- Crewel (Embroidery)—A sharp needle with a long, oval eye. Use for smooth- to medium-textured surfaces.

- Chenille—A long-eyed needle with a sharp point. Use for working heavy threads, fabrics, and silk ribbon embroidery.

- Darner—A long, strong needle with a large eye, good for assembly work, wool darning, and working with heavy threads and fabrics.

- Millinery (Straw Needle)—A long, narrow needle with a small, round eye, it is the same thickness from end to end. Excellent for making French Knots.

- Sharps—A fine, yet strong, round-eyed needle that is rather short. Excellent for fine embroidery and hand sewing.

- Tapestry—A large, oval-eyed needle with a rounded point. Use for working pulled and drawn work, and for silk ribbon embroidery.

Threads The choice of thread is always governed by your choice of fabric and the project in mind. Learn to experiment with different threads and yarns to find which types work best with different types of fabrics.

- Brazilian embroidery thread—A twisted, rayon embroidery thread with a good sheen. Use short lengths because it tends to knot up. Avoid kinks in the thread by dampening a cloth with water then drawing the thread over it before using.

- Coton à Broder—A single, highly twisted thread with a shiny finish.

- Crewel yarn—Very fine, three-stranded wool. The strands can be separated and used singly for embroidery.

- Filo-Floss—A soft, loosely twisted, six-stranded pure silk thread. It can be separated like cotton floss, and then used singly or in varying multiple strands as desired.

- Linen thread—A strong, highly twisted, single thread with a slight sheen.

- Marlett—A very shiny viscose thread that comes in loose strands, which can be separated for finer work.

- Metallics—Any thread with glitter and shine is referred to as a metallic. Pure gold and silver threads tarnish and need careful handling, but many imitations are available. Keep a good variety on hand for couching and weaving techniques. I prefer machine-embroidery metallics because they are smoother and pass more easily through fabric.

- Natesh—Rayon thread with a wonderful sheen; double it up for Victorian crazy quilt stitching.

- Perle cotton—A single, low luster thread with a sharply defined twist. Available plain or dyed, it is often used for crochet and is wonderful for creating texture in embroidery; it is available in sizes 3, 5, and 8 (the thinnest).

Persian wool—A three-stranded wool, thicker than crewel but thinner than tapestry, that can be easily separated. Use for textural work in pictorial crazy quilting.

Silk buttonhole twist—An exquisite thread that will surely spoil you! The silk takes on a special sheen that stands up to lots of wear, plus it feeds through the fabric easily. I use it exclusively for Victorian needlework. One strand is equivalent to three strands of embroidery floss. For a 200+ color range, try the variety of Kanagawa silk threads.

Silk ribbon—The bias silk ribbon retains its color and comes in a large range of colors. It can be used in a variety of ways, including for embroidery, punch needle, and covering seams. It creates wonderful texture and is very pliable and soft.

Silk Sewing Thread—A single strand of very fine thread that's used for fine heirloom sewing. Try combining this thread with other threads.

Soie d'Alger—Seven-stranded silk thread that can be separated or used as is.

Stranded Embroidery Floss—A six-stranded cotton thread that easily separates allowing you to use the strands one at a time or in multiples.

Tapestry wool—A thick, bulky yarn, traditionally used for needlepoint. It can be used in punch needle or embroidery. Try combining it with metallics for variety.

Ver a Soie—Twisted silk thread similar to buttonhole twist.

Stitching Instructions Working from the back of the fabric, insert the threaded needle into the fabric 2″–3″ from the starting point of the first stitch, then work a few running stitches to secure the thread end. The running stitches can be covered as you complete the embroidery stitches, securing the thread end. The running stitches can be taken out after the design is stitched. Rethread the needle, then work the needle through the backs of the completed stitches.

Silk Ribbon Embroidery The secret to good silk ribbon embroidery is to keep the stitches loose and even. Silk ribbon embroidery is dimensional and fast. Here are a few tips to make your stitching easy and successful:

Threading Up the Ribbon—Remember, silk ribbon is delicate and will fray on the edges. Use a short length (12″–16″).

Needle Eye Lock—Thread the ribbon through the eye of the needle. Pierce one end of the ribbon (centered ¼″ from the end) with the point of the needle. Pull the long end of the ribbon and lock it into the eye of the needle.

Soft knot—Make the needle eye lock. Grasp the end of the ribbon, then form a circle with the end of the ribbon and the point of the needle (A). Pierce the end of the ribbon with a short running stitch (B). Pull the needle and ribbon through the running stitch to form a soft knot.

A

B

Ribbon manipulation—If the ribbon is pulled too tight or it twists too much, it will just look like a heavy thread. Most stitches depend on the ribbon being flat. Use your free thumb to hold the ribbon flat against the fabric. Keep your thumb in place while you stitch, and tighten the ribbon over your thumb. This will remove any twists. (A large needle or a knitting stitch holder can be used instead of your thumb.)

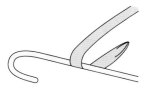

Adjusting the ribbon—Sometimes the ribbon will fold up on itself as it passes through the fabric, and it has to be adjusted, so the full width of the ribbon shows. Hold the ribbon flat under the free thumb and slide the needle under the ribbon, then gently slide the needle back and forth (from the thumb to the needle hole in the fabric).

Correct needles—The heavier the fabric, the larger the eye of the needle you should use. Above all, use a chenille needle when piercing through fabric; use a tapestry needle for wrapping or whipping.

Hoops A hoop in which your thumb and fingers reach comfortably to the middle seems to be the best (6″–7″). I find that a wooden hoop with the inner circle wrapped in yarn holds well and is especially useful when stitching velvet or high-nap fabrics.

Insert the fabric into the hoop by laying the area to be embroidered over the inner ring. Align fabric so the grain is straight and the surface is smooth. Add the top circle and adjust the tension screw if needed. Always remove your work from the hoop when you are not embroidering, so the fabric isn't marked or creased.

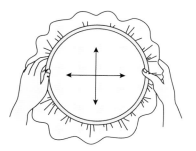

If odd fabric shapes are problematic, first sew the shape onto a large square of support fabric, basting the shape into place with small Running Stitches. Insert into the hoop. Working from the wrong side of the fabric, cut away the support fabric from inside the odd shape. The fabric is now ready for embroidery work. Be careful not to stitch through the support fabric. After stitching, remove the basting stitches.

Frames Used for large pieces of embroidery. The basic frame consists of two rollers (top and bottom) that have strips of tape or canvas webbing across the bar length. To support the base fabric, first zigzag stitch a $1/2''$ hem on the edges. Fine base fabrics almost always require support for the edges; try stitching bias tape or attaching strips of support fabric to the edges.

Mark the center of both rollers and the top and bottom edges of the base fabric. Attach the fabric's edges, using lacing stitches, to the tape or canvas strips on the rollers. Match the center points and work outward from the center. Roll any excess fabric around one roller. The flat side supports hold the rollers in place with pegs or screws. The overall stitching area also depends on the length of the side supports used. Attach the flat side supports, then roll the bars to stretch the fabric.

Using strong thread, lace the fabric's edges evenly to the flat side supports. Tighten the lace on each side and knot the thread ends firmly. An added advantage of working with a frame is that it can be secured on a stand if needed, allowing the needleworker to use both hands while working the stitches.

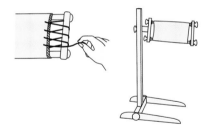

Thimble The small indentations on the tip hold and guide the needle into place, as well as protect your fingers! It should fit snugly.

Scissors Make sure they are sharp, strong, and have narrow, pointed blades for precise cutting when needed.

Washing the Finished Work Use lukewarm water and pure soap flakes. Gently squeeze any excess water from the fabric, then rinse thoroughly. Squeeze again by hand, then leave until partially dry before blocking and pressing.

Blocking and Pressing After the finished work is washed, measure a piece of graph paper the same size as the base fabric. Place the fabric right side up on the paper and, using the grid lines, pull the fabric into shape. Pin in position with rustproof pushpins. Cover with a damp cloth, or acid-free tissue paper, and let dry. If the embroidery is hard to block, or blocking isn't required, place it right side down on a well-padded board (use toweling for ribbon work) and press lightly using a damp pressing cloth. Do not flatten the embroidery.

Embellishments Don't be afraid to collage different techniques and materials together.

- Beads and Nymo beading thread—this thread will not deteriorate with time or cleaning, and it is virtually invisible within the embroidery.

- Buttons

- Metal findings

Useful Tips

- Test your threads, yarns, or ribbons for color-fastness. Hang them over the edge of a glass of water and leave submerged for ten minutes. Remove and place on a white paper towel or nonabrasive fabric, press the towel with your fingers, then open and check for color stains.

- Work a small trial piece first to test the thickness of the threads, the stitches, and the appropriateness of the fabric.

- Cut more fabric than you will need. The rule of thumb is 2″ extra all around.

- Avoid knots on the back of your finished work. They cause bumps and lumps, and show up as a shiny spots when they have been pressed. Whenever you can, run the starting end through the fabric under the area to be worked, then finish on the wrong side by running the other end under the stitches just worked.

- Cut clothing patterns larger than you'll need in order to insert the fabric into the hoop or frame. After the seams are sewn, work some of the embroidery over the seamlines for a more professional look.

- Press your finished work. For thread work, press from the wrong side with a damp pressing cloth on a padded board. For silk ribbon work, use a dry iron and a terry towel for padding.

Stitches

Algerian Eye Stitch

LEFT-HANDED

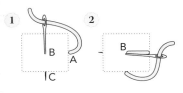

1 Come up at A, go down at B, then up at C.

2 Point B becomes the pivot point for the stitches.

3–6 Continue inserting the needle at point B and forming the stitches along the designated line until the stitch is finished.

Variations

RIGHT-HANDED

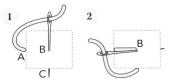

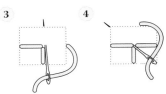

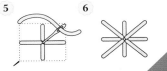

23

Arrowhead Stitch

1 Come up at A, go down at B, then up at C.

2–3 On the return pass, work the stitches in the same way, filling in the spaces. Use this stitch on its own or stack it to make a filler stitch.

Variation

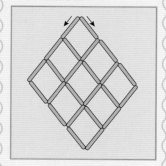

LEFT-HANDED

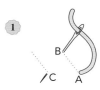

RIGHT-HANDED

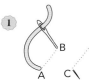

Arrowhead Stitch—Stacked

1 Come up at A, go down at B, then up at C.

2 Go down at B and up at D.

3 Continue until each arrowhead is completed, keeping the stitches evenly spaced.

Leaf

1 Mark the shape as a guide. Come up at A, go down at B, then up at C.

2–4 Continue working in this manner, keeping the stitches very close.

LEFT-HANDED

1   2

3   1

2   3

4

RIGHT-HANDED

1   2

3   1

2   3

4

Backstitch

1 Come up at A, take a small backward stitch, go down at B, then up at C.

2–4 Always move the needle forward under the fabric and come up one stitch length ahead (D), ready to take another stitch.

Backstitch—Star Stitch

LEFT-HANDED

1 Come up at A and go down at B (point B becomes the center pivot of the stitch). Continue stitching the spokes (6 or 8), keeping them of equal length and spaced evenly.

2–3 Connect the spokes with Straight Stitches on the edges.

RIGHT-HANDED

Backstitch—Threaded

LEFT-HANDED

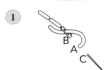

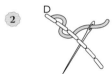

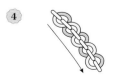

1 Come up at A, take a small Backstitch to B, then come up at C.

2 Work the Backstitches to the length desired. Come up at D with a contrasting thread. Slide the needle under the Backstitches, alternating above and below the row without catching the fabric.

3–4 Interweave another contrasting thread to complete the loops.

RIGHT-HANDED

28

Basque Stitch

RIGHT-HANDED

1 Work this stitch along 2 parallel lines. Come up at A, go down at B, then up at C.

2 Slide the needle under the stitch between A and B, to the right of C (to the left of C if left-handed).

3 Loop the thread around the stitch again, bringing the needle tip over the thread.

4 Pull the thread to form a knot. Go down at D, and come up at E to continue with the next stitch.

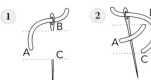

Bosnian Stitch

1 Come up at A, go down at B, then up at C.

2–3 On the return pass, work the diagonal stitches, filling in the spaces.

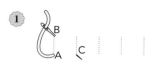

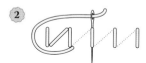

Bradford Rose

1 Form the rose center with a French (page 94) or Colonial Knot (page 63).

2 Working around the knot, stitch 3 curved Whip Stitches (page 179).

3–4 Work 4 to 5 more curved Whip Stitches in a circle around the previous round. For variety, use dark ribbon in the center fading to light ribbon around the edges.

Braid Stitch

LEFT-HANDED

1 Come up at A, go down at B, then up at C. Slide the needle under the Straight Stitch between A and B, go down again at D (as close to C as possible, but not into it), and emerge at E.

2–3 Slide the needle under the Straight Stitch again. Go down at F, and up at G.

4–5 Slide the needle under the Chain Stitches and continue with the next stitch.

RIGHT-HANDED

Bullion Rose

1 For the rose center, work 3 Bullion Stitches (page 35) of equal length to form a triangle.

2–4 Work a Bullion Stitch to wrap around one corner of the triangle. Lengthen the knots as needed, so each knot curls around the others. Continue stitching knots around the triangle until the rose is formed.

LEFT-HANDED

RIGHT-HANDED

1

2

3

4

1

2

3

4

Bullion Rosebud

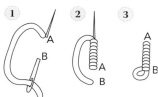

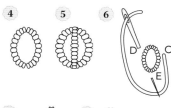

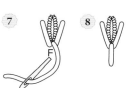

1 Come up at A; pull the thread through. Go down at B. Come up again at A.

2 Wrap the needle several times to fill the desired length. Hold the wraps firmly and pull the needle through, away from you.

3 Pull the wraps toward you and anchor the bullion by going back down at B.

4 If you are making 2 bullions, work the stitches so they curve toward each other.

5 If you are making 3 bullions, work the center bullion first, then add the right and left Bullion Stitches so they curve toward the center.

6 Come up at C, go down at D and up at E; pull the thread through.

7–8 Go down at F.

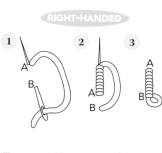

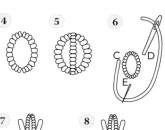

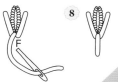

Bullion Stitch

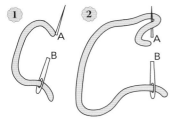

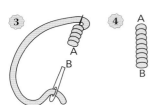

1 Decide the width of the stitch, then come up at A. Pull the thread through. Go down at B. Come up again at A.

2 Raise the tip of the needle by holding it in your hand and putting pressure on top of the needle eye. Wrap the needle with the thread; pull the wrap firmly down toward the fabric.

3 Work the desired number of wraps until the wraps are the same width as the space from A to B. Pull the wraps firmly into place.

4 Hold the wraps and pull the needle through the wraps. Pull the thread through, holding firmly, and pull away from you in order to tighten the knot. Go back into B to put the bullion into place.

RIGHT-HANDED

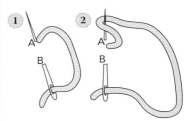

Buttonhole Stitch

LEFT-HANDED

1 Come up at A, hold the thread down with your thumb, go down at B, then up at C.

2–3 Bring the needle tip over the thread and pull into place. Repeat.

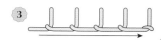

Buttonhole Stitch—Circle

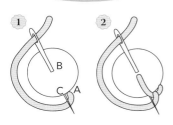

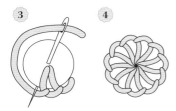

1 Draw a circle the desired size of the flower. Bring the needle up at A (the outside of the circle). Go down at center B and come up at C, to the right of A (to the left of A if left-handed). Make sure the needle is over the thread; pull firmly.

2–4 Continue around the circle until it is filled.

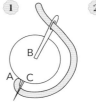

Buttonhole Stitch—Closed

LEFT-HANDED

1 Come up at A, hold the thread down with your thumb, go down at B, then up at C.

2 Bring the needle tip over the thread and pull into place. Go down at B and up at D to form the second side stitch.

3 Go down at E and up at F to begin the next stitch.

RIGHT-HANDED

Buttonhole Stitch—Detached

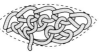

1 Draw a leaf outline onto your fabric. Work a Chain Stitch (page 46) along the top of the leaf. Work a row of Buttonhole Stitch (page 36) loops under the Chain Stitch. Keep the loops rather loose.

2 Once at the other side, take the thread back to the opposite side. Start another row of loops.

3 Continue to the desired width, filling the designated shape.

$\mathcal{B}$uttonhole Stitch—Knotted

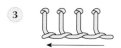

1 Come up at A and form a loop, wrapping the thread around your thumb. Slip the needle under the front of the loop.

2–3 Work the loop onto the needle. Insert the needle at B and emerge at C; form a neat knot by gently tightening the loop before pulling the needle through the fabric.

Buttonhole Stitch—Triangle

LEFT-HANDED

①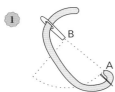

②

1 Draw a quarter-circle shape. Come up at A (at the outer left corner, out right corner if left-handed). Go back down at B, bringing the needle up close to A. Loop the thread under the needle; pull through.

2 Continue making stitches to fill the area. End with a Catch Stitch.

Variation

RIGHT-HANDED

①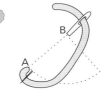

②

Buttonhole Stitch—Up and Down

LEFT-HANDED

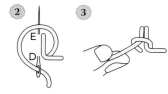

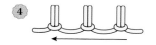

1 Come up at A and hold the thread down with your thumb. Go down at B then up at C, bringing the needle tip over the thread.

2–4 Go down at D then up at E. Gently pull the thread until the loop is tightened.

RIGHT-HANDED

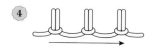

Cable Stitch

1 Come up at A, go down at B, then up at C (the center of the desired stitch length) keeping the working thread below the needle tip.

2–3 Work the next stitch in the same manner, keeping the thread above the needle tip. Stitch along the designated line, using small, even stitches and alternating the position of the thread above or below the needle.

LEFT-HANDED

RIGHT-HANDED

43

Cast-On Stitch Flower

LEFT-HANDED

1 Come up at A. Take a small Backstitch toward A and leave the needle in the fabric.

2 Grasp the emerging thread in one hand and lay it over the index finger of your other hand (which faces toward you).

3 Twist your finger under the emerging thread so that the thread coming out of A lies on top.

4 Slip the loop onto the needle (cast on). Pull the thread tight and slip the loop down the needle toward the fabric.

5 Continue to cast on more loops until you have the desired length. Hold the cast-on stitches, and pull the needle and thread through the stitches.

6–7 Go down at B and pull the thread through.

RIGHT-HANDED

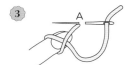

Chain Rose

1 Mark a circle the size of the desired rose. Come up at A, go down at B, then up at C, bringing the needle tip over the ribbon.

2–3 Repeat this stitch, making a continuous chain and working in a counterclockwise direction (clockwise if left-handed) to fill the circle.

Chain Stitch

1–2 Come up at A and form a loop. Go down at B (as close to A as possible but not into it) and emerge at C, bringing the needle tip over the thread. Repeat this stitch to make a chain.

1

2

1

2

Chain Stitch—Cable

1 Come up at A and wrap the thread once around the needle.

2–3 Go down at B then up at C, bringing the needle tip over the thread. Pull the thread taut after each stitch.

Chain Stitch—Crochet

1 Come up at A, go down at B, then come up at A again.

2–3 Remove the needle from the thread. With a crochet hook, reach under the Straight Stitch and work up a series of Chain Stitches. Work each to the desired length. Rethread the needle and anchor to the back. The Chain Stitch can be tacked down with another thread.

Variation

①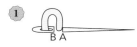

②

③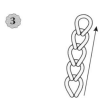

①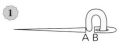

②

③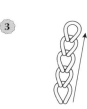

Chain Stitch—Detached Twisted

1 Come up at A and form a loop. Go down at B, even with and to the left of A (to the right of A if left-handed), then up at C, bringing the needle tip over the thread.

2–3 Go down at D, making a small anchor stitch at the bottom of the loop.

1

2

3

1

2

3

Chain Stitch—Flower; Detached

1 Come up at A. Go down (as close to A as possible but not into it) and come up at B. Make sure the needle lies over the loop; pull through.

2 Fill in with Buttonhole Stitches (page 36). End by taking the thread just over the last loop.

Chain Stitch—Magic

1 Thread the needle with 2 contrasting threads. Come up at A and form a loop. Go down at B (as close to A as possible but not into it) and emerge at C, looping only one thread under the needle tip. The first thread will appear as a single chain stitch and the second will disappear behind the fabric.

2-4 Repeat, working the second thread under the needle tip. Continue stitching, alternating the first and second threads for the loops.

Chain Stitch—Open

1 Work this stitch along 2 parallel lines. Come up at A and form a loop. Go down at B even with and to the right of A (to the left of A if left-handed), then up at C, bringing the needle tip over the thread. Leave the loop loose.

2–3 Go down at D, over the loop, and emerge at E for the next stitch. Anchor the stitch end with two catch stitches.

Chain Stitch—Rosette

LEFT-HANDED

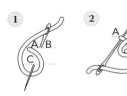

1 Work this stitch along 2 parallel lines. Come up at A and form a loop. Go down at B, even with and to the left of A (to the right of A if left-handed), taking a small, slanting stitch; then come up at C, bringing the needle tip over the thread.

2 Pull the needle through, and pass the needle tip under the top thread at A.

3–4 Go down at D, then up at E. Continue the stitches.

RIGHT-HANDED

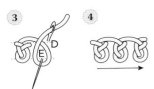

Stitch—Russian

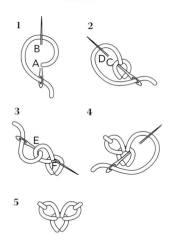

1 Come up at A and form a loop. Go down (as close to A as possible but not into it) and emerge at B, bringing the needle tip over the thread.

2 Go down at C, form a loop, and come up at D.

3 Go down at E to make an anchor stitch, then come up at F.

4–5 Repeat the steps to form the next looped stitch in the same manner.

Variation

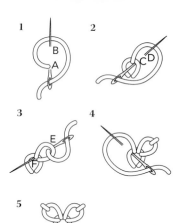

Chain Stitch—Spiny

1 Come up at A and form a loop. Go down at B, then up at C, bringing the needle tip over the thread.

2 Go down at D, making a Straight Stitch to the desired length, then up at E.

3–4 Go down at F and emerge at G, bringing the needle tip over the thread to continue the next stitch.

Chain Stitch—Twisted

LEFT-HANDED

1 Work this stitch along a line. Come up at A along the designated line and form a loop. Go down at B, slightly to the left of A (to the right of A if left-handed), and take a small, slanting stitch to C, bringing the needle tip over the thread.

2–3 Repeat this stitch for a continuous row.

RIGHT-HANDED

Chain Stitch—Whipped

1 Make a row of continuous Chain Stitches (page 46).

2–3 Using a blunt needle, come up at A and wrap the ribbon or thread around each individual Chain Stitch by bringing the needle under each stitch from the top. If using ribbon, keep it flat.

(1)

(2)

(3)

(1)

(2)

Chain Stitch—Zigzag

1 Come up at A and form a loop. Go down at B (as close to A as possible, but not into it) then up at C, bringing the needle tip over the thread.

2–3 Form another loop and go down at D, piercing the lower curve of the first loop to keep it in position, then emerge at E.

LEFT-HANDED

RIGHT-HANDED

Chevron Stitch

1 Work this stitch along 2 parallel lines. Come up at A, go down at B, then up at C (the center of the stitch).

2 Make a Straight Stitch the desired length to D, then come up at E.

3–4 Go down at F (equal to the length of AB) then up at G. Continue working, alternating from one side to the other.

LEFT-HANDED

①

②

③

④

RIGHT-HANDED

①

②

③

④

Chinese Knot (Peking Knot)

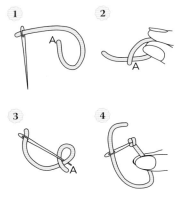

1 Come up at A and loop the thread.

2 Hold the loop down with your thumb and finger. Pick up the loop and flip it over so the thread coming out of A is on the top.

3 Insert the needle inside the loop (as close to A as possible but not into it).

4–5 Pull the knot firmly into place. Holding the thread taut with your thumb, push the needle through to the back.

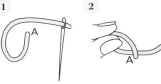

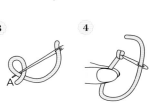

Chinese Knot —Looped

1–4 Work the Chinese Knot up to the point of pulling the thread through to the back of the fabric.

5 Hold the loop at the desired length with your thumb; pull the thread through to the back. Tighten; the loop should sit on top of the knot.

LEFT-HANDED

1

2

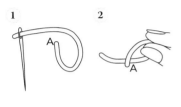

3

4

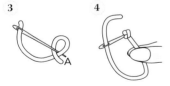

5

RIGHT-HANDED

1

2

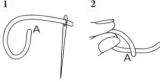

3

4

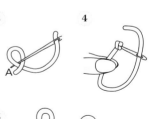

5

Christine's Blossom (Christine Simpson)

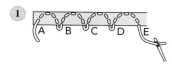

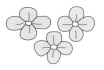

1 Use 3mm-wide satin ribbon, matching thread, and a fine needle. Start Running Stitches (page 150) at A and create ½"-wide arches. Make sure the thread loops over the edges at B, C, and D.

2–3 Finish at E and gently gather. Four little petals will form. Join the edges and sew into place. You can add a bead to the center.

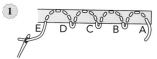

Colonial Knot

1 Come up at A. Work the thread to form a figure 8-shaped loop, starting over the needle head and ending under the needle tip.

2–4 Hold the needle upright and pull the thread firmly around the needle. Insert the needle at B (as close to A as possible, but not into it). Hold the knot in place until the needle is pulled completely through the fabric.

(1)

(2)

(3)

(4)

(1)

(2)

(3)

(4)

Concertina Rose

1

1 Thread the needle (using thread that matches the ribbon) and knot the end. Fold the ribbon at a right angle in the center.

2 Fold the horizontal section of the ribbon over to the left. Then fold the ribbon up and over from the bottom. The folds will take on a square look. Keep folding from right to left, top to bottom, left to right, and bottom to top until the ribbon is used up.

3–4 Grasp both ends in one hand and pull gently down on either end until a rose is formed. With the knotted thread, go down and up through the top 2 or 3 times. Tightly wrap the ribbon ends at the base. Make a knot, cut the thread, and leave a 6″ tail to sew down later.

2

2

3

3

4

4

Coral Stitch

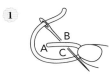

1–3 Work the stitch along a designated line. Come up at A and lay the thread along the designated line. Bring the needle down at a right angle to the thread at B, and up at C, bringing the needle tip over the thread.

LEFT-HANDED

1

2

3

RIGHT-HANDED

1

2

3

65

Coral Stitch—Zigzag

1 Work this stitch along 2 parallel lines. On the top line, come up at A, go down at B, then up at C, bringing the needle tip over the thread.

2 Reverse the loop on the lower line, moving it slightly to the left (to the right if left-handed). Go down at D and emerge at E, bringing the needle tip over the thread.

3–4 Continue with the next stitch.

1

2

3

4

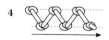

1

2

3

4

Couched Rose

1 Come up at A and form a U shape. Go down at B, keeping the ribbon loose. Couch the U (page 68).

2–3 Come up at C and work around the U center, couching the ribbon down to form the rose.

This rose works best with 4mm- or 7mm-wide ribbon.

LEFT-HANDED

1

2

3

RIGHT-HANDED

1

2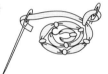

3

Couching Stitch

1–2 Couching is a decorative way to hold a long (placed) thread in position. Mark a line the designated length of the Couching Stitch. Position the thread along the designated line. With either matching or contrasting thread or ribbon, come up at A and go down at B, wrapping a small, tight stitch over the placed thread at regular intervals.

①

②

①

②

68

Cretan Stitch

1 Work this stitch along two parallel lines. Come up at A, go down at B, then up at C, taking a downward vertical stitch and bringing the needle tip over the thread.

2–3 Go down at D, then up at E.

①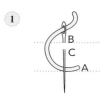

②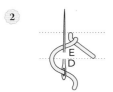

③

①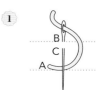

②

③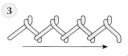

69

Cretan Stitch—Decorative

LEFT-HANDED

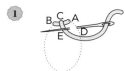

1 Mark the shape to guide the stitches. Come up at A to the left of center (to the right if left-handed), go down at B, then come up at C, in the center of the stitch. Go down at D then emerge at E, bringing the needle tip over the thread.

2–3 Continue stitching from side to side until the shape is completely filled.

RIGHT-HANDED

Cross Stitch

1 Come up at A, go down at B, then up at C, making a row of even, slanted stitches.

2–3 On the return pass, cross over the first stitches to form X's.

LEFT-HANDED

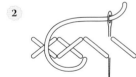

RIGHT-HANDED

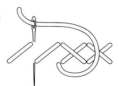

Cross Stitch—Flower

1 Come up at A and go down at B. Cross over the stitch with an equal-sized stitch from C to D.

2 Come up again at A and cross over to B. Come up again at C to start the next stitch, weaving the thread through the stitches.

3–4 Continue weaving to make a larger decorative Cross-Stitch flower.

(1)

(2)

(3)

(4)

(1)

(2)

(3)

(4)

Cross Stitch—St. George

LEFT-HANDED

RIGHT-HANDED

1 Come up at A, go down at B, then up at C, making a row of evenly spaced Running Stitches (page 150).

2–3 On the return pass, come up at D, go down at E, then emerge at F, crossing each Running Stitch with a vertical stitch of equal length.

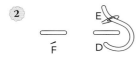

Crown Stitch

1 Come up at A, go down at B, then up at C, bringing the needle tip over the thread. Keep the stitch loose to form a slight curve.

2 Go down at D, then up at E, bringing the needle tip next to the working thread.

3 Go down at F, then up at G.

4–5 Go down at H, to the left of the center Straight Stitch.

1

1

2

2

3

3

4

4

5

5

Double Knot

LEFT-HANDED

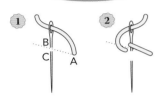

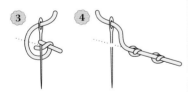

1 Work this stitch along a designated line. Come up at A, go down at B, then up at C.

2–3 Slide the needle under the stitch and loop the thread around the stitch, bringing the needle tip over the threads.

4–5 Pull the thread to form the knot, and continue with the next stitch.

RIGHT-HANDED

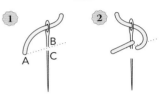

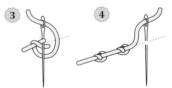

Elly's Wire Ribbon Pansy (Elly Sienkiewicz)

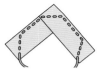

1 Cut 2 lengths of ribbon, each 4 ribbon widths long. Overlap the ribbons at a 90° angle. Add a Running Stitch (page 150) along the ribbons' edges.

2 Gather the ribbons to form a back petal. Wrap the thread around the ribbon ends to secure. Repeat the process for a second back petal.

3 Cut one length of ribbon 12 ribbon widths long and fold into 3 equal sections. Add a Running Stitch along the ribbon edge.

4 Gather the ribbon, forming 3 front petals. Wrap the thread around the ribbon ends to secure.

5 Secure the 2 back petals to the front 3-petal unit to create the pansy. Add a bead, ribbon, or embroidery thread for the center.

Ermine Stitch

1 Make 2 parallel lines to start. Come up at A, go down at B, then come up at C.

2 Go down at D, then come up at E.

3–4 Go down at F to complete the stitch.

Variation

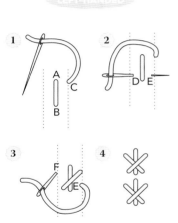

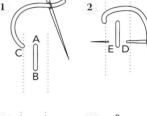

Eyelet Flower

1 Gently pierce a hole in the fabric with an awl. Make a small Running Stitch (page 150) just outside the hole. Take the needle through to the back.

2 Make a Satin Stitch (page 153) to cover the edge of the hole. Keep an even tension, and cover the Running Stitch. Finish the Satin Stitch and take the thread to the back. End by running the thread under the stitches to secure.

3 Work four Straight Stitches (page 167) on each side (or 4 Lazy Daisy Stitches, page 111).

Eyelets Freeform

1 Gently pierce a hole in the fabric with an awl. Come up at A, then go down into the center hole.

2 Come up again and work Straight Stitches around the center hole. Pull firmly to keep the hole open.

1

1

2

2

Feather Stitch

1 Come up at A, go down at B—even with and to the left of A (to the right of A if left-handed)—then up at C.

2–3 Alternate the stitches back and forth, working them downward in a vertical column.

Variation

Work the Double Feather Stitch in the same manner, but complete 2 stitches before alternating the direction.

LEFT-HANDED

1

2

3

RIGHT-HANDED

1

2

3

80

Feather Stitch—Chained

1 Work this stitch along 2 parallel lines. Come up at A and form a loop. Go down at B (as close to A as possible, but not into it), and emerge at C, bringing the needle tip over the thread.

2–3 Go down at D, making a slanted Straight Stitch the desired length. Come up at E and continue working the next stitch. Always work the Straight Stitches to form a regular zigzag pattern.

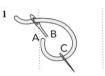

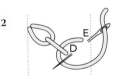

Feather Stitch—Closed

LEFT-HANDED

1 Work this stitch along 2 parallel lines. Come up at A, go down at B, then up at C, bringing the needle tip over the thread.

2–3 Go down at D, then up at E, bringing the needle tip over the thread.

RIGHT-HANDED

Feather Stitch—Leaf

1 Draw a leaf outline onto your fabric. Start at the top of the leaf with the first Feather Stitch (page 80). Alternate the stitches left and right, working them downward in a vertical column.

2 Work out to the outside lines. These stitches are uneven and meant to be freeform. This stitch can also be worked in multiple layers of color.

Variation

Fern Leaf Stitch

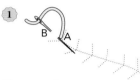

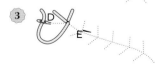

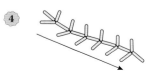

1 Mark a line the designated length of the fern leaf. Come up at A, go down at B (making a Straight Stitch) then come up again at A.

2 Go down at C, then come up again at A.

3–4 Go down at D, keeping the length of the Straight Stitches consistent with the first set. Come up at E, and continue with the next stitch, forming the stitch along the designated line.

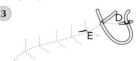

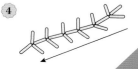

Fishbone Stitch

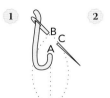

1 Draw a leaf outline onto your fabric. Come up at A on the center line. Go down at B, then back up at C, keeping the thread on the right side of the needle (on the left if left-handed).

2 Pull the thread through. With the thread on the left (on the right if left-handed), go down at D, then up at E.

3–4 Continue stitching to form the leaf.

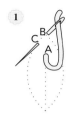

Variations

Fishbone Stitch (Open)

Five-Petal Gathered Flower

LEFT-HANDED

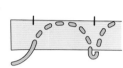

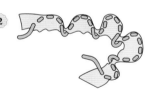

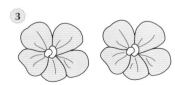

1 For ⅝"-wide ribbon, cut a length 7³⁄₈" long. Mark at 1³⁄₈" intervals. Using a Running Stitch (page 150), make 5 half-circles. Make sure to loop under the ribbon edge at the bottom of each half-curve, to ensure that the thread will gather easily.

2–3 Gently pull the thread, gathering the ribbon into 5 petals. When the petals are pulled into place, sew the 2 ribbon ends together and trim away any excess. Add French Knots (page 94) or Pistil Stitches (page 140) to the center.

RIGHT-HANDED

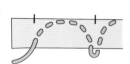

Flat Stitch

LEFT-HANDED

1 Mark 2 lines down the center of the shape as a guide for the stitches. Come up at A, go down at B, slip the needle tip under the fabric, then up at C.

2–3 Continue working, keeping the stitches close together and alternating from side to side. Each new stitch will overlap the base of the previous stitch.

RIGHT-HANDED

①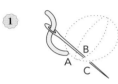

①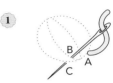

②

②

③

③

Fly Stitch

LEFT-HANDED

(1)

(2)

(3)

1 Come up at A, go down at B—even with and to the right of A (to the left of A if left-handed)—then up at C, bringing the needle tip over the thread.

2–3 Draw the thread gently through the fabric. Go down at D, forming a catch stitch.

This stitch may be worked singly or stitched in rows.

Variation

RIGHT-HANDED

(1)

(2)

(3)

Fly Stitch—Circle

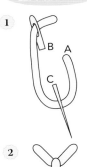

LEFT-HANDED

1

2

3

1 Come up at A and pull the thread through. Make a loop, go down at B, then come up at C, bringing the needle tip over the thread; pull the stitch into place.

2 Go down at D to finish.

3 Continue making stitches to form a circle.

Variations

RIGHT-HANDED

1

2

3

Stitch—Dandelion Seed Pod

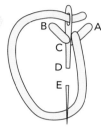

1

2

1 Work Step 1, page 89.

2 Hold the thread to the left (to the right if left-handed). Make a small Lazy Daisy Stitch (page 111). Go down at D, then up at E. Pull stitch into place, making sure the needle lies over the thread. Anchor with a catch stitch at F.

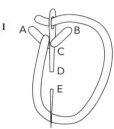

1

2

Fly Stitch—Leaf

1 Draw a leaf outline onto your fabric. Make a Fly Stitch: come up at A, go down at B, up at C, and down at D.

2 Work a series of freeform Fly Stitches, going to the outside edges of the leaf. The center, or spine, of the leaf will be where the Catch Stitch (D) of the Fly Stitch is placed.

1
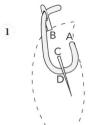

2

1
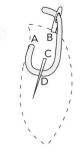

2

Folded Rosebud

1 Make a 90° angle 1″ from the end of a piece of ribbon.

2 Make 3 tight rolls. Stitch to anchor tightly at the base. Make a petal by folding the ribbon back and down.

3 Wrap this petal around the rolled ribbon, angling the petal toward the base of the bud. Stitch at the base, and secure.

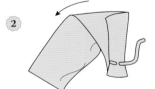

Freeform Flower

1

2

1 Use narrow ribbon, ⅛" to ¼" wide, cut in 3" lengths for tiny flowers. Use wider ribbon, ½" to 1" wide, cut in 4" lengths, for larger flowers. Fold both ends under and baste along one long edge.

2 Pull the thread to gather tightly and knot the thread ends. Whip Stitch the folded ribbon ends together. Leave a thread tail to sew down later.

1

2

French Knot

1 Come up at A and wrap the thread twice around the needle.

2–3 Holding the thread taut, go down at B (as close to A as possible, but not into it). Hold the knot in place until the needle is completely through the fabric.

1

1

2

2

3

3

French Knot Flower

LEFT-HANDED

1 Use a short length of ribbon (12″). Come up at A. Wrap the ribbon once around the needle.

RIGHT-HANDED

2 Go back into the fabric (as close to A as possible but not into it). Do not pull the knot tight. Pull the needle and ribbon gently to the back. Leave a very loose French Knot on the fabric.

3 With thread, come up in the center of the ribbon knot and make a French Knot to anchor the ribbon (forming the center of the flower). I like to stitch several ribbon French Knots and then come back to anchor them with thread French Knots.

French Knot Loop Stitch

LEFT-HANDED

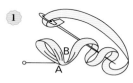

1 Come up at A, make a loop, and hold it in place with a straight pin. Form a French Knot center by wrapping the ribbon twice around the needle. Go down at B (close to the pin).

2 Gently pull the knot into place. Keep the ribbon taut while pulling the needle through to the back.

RIGHT-HANDED

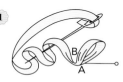

Gathered Ribbon Flower

LEFT-HANDED

(1)

(2)

(3)

(4)

(5)

1 Cut a 15″ length of 7mm silk ribbon. Using Nymo thread or a matching color thread, sew a line of small, even Running Stitches (page 150) along one edge of the ribbon.

2 Evenly gather the Running Stitches until the ribbon is half its original length. Fold the end down and secure with a knot.

3 Draw a flower outline onto the fabric. Anchor the edge of the ribbon to the center of the flower shape using 2 small stitches.

4–5 Fold the ribbon around the center. Stitch it in place every ¹⁄₈″ or so. Continue around in a spiral, until the shape is filled. To finish, turn the ribbon edge under and attach it with 2 small stitches. Go to the back and make a knot.

RIGHT-HANDED

(1)

(2)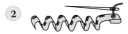

(3)

(4)

(5)

Granito

1.
2.
3.
4.

1 Come up at A and go down at B.

2 Come back up at A in the same hole. Pull the thread through. Loop the thread to the left and go back down at B (through the same hole); pull through and position the thread on the left.

3 Come back up at A and loop the thread to the right. Go back down at B.

4 Add extra stitches to make a larger Granito. The small bud shape may look different based on the number of stitches.

Variation

1.
2.
3.
4.

Head of the Bull Stitch

LEFT-HANDED

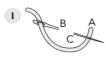

1 Come up at A, go down at B, then up at C, bringing the needle tip over the thread.

2 Go down at D to the right of the working thread, (to the left if left-handed) then up at E, bringing the needle tip over the thread.

3–4 Take a small stitch at F to anchor the loop.

RIGHT-HANDED

LEFT- AND RIGHT-HANDED

1 Use the Japanese Ribbon Stitch (page 106) and 4mm-wide ribbon for base petals and 7mm-wide ribbon for shadow and outer bowl petals.

2 For base petals, start from the center using the darkest shade. The petals will curve upward.

3 Add the shadow petals using a lighter shade.

4 Add 4 outer bowl petals, keeping them loose. Add a few more petals inside the outer bowl petals.

5 Work French Knots (page 94) to fill in the center. Add 3 or 4 shorter petals in the center front. Add a couple of base petals if necessary.

Herringbone Stitch

1 Come up at A, go down at B, then up at C.

2–3 Go down at D, then up at E. Continue working, alternating from top to bottom.

LEFT-HANDED

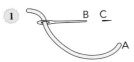

RIGHT-HANDED

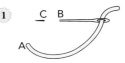

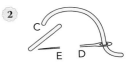

Herringbone Stitch—Laced

LEFT-HANDED

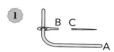

1 Come up at A, go down at B, then up at C.

2–3 Slide the needle under the slanted stitch. Go down at D, then up at E.

4–5 With a contrasting thread, come up at 1. Slide the thread under the first crossing of slanted stitches. Work it over, under, and over the slanted stitches. Work it under the thread at 1, then over and under at the same crossing, bringing the thread to the lower crossing.

RIGHT-HANDED

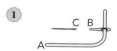

Holbein Stitch

LEFT-HANDED

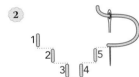

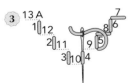

1 Come up at A and go down at B, making a Straight Stitch of the desired length.

2 Continue, making a V shape of even, vertical stitches.

3–4 On the return pass, work the horizontal Straight Stitches in the same way, filling in the spaces.

RIGHT-HANDED

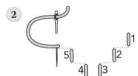

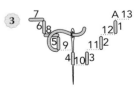

Iris Stitch

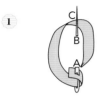

1 Form a loose Lazy Daisy: come up at A, then form a loop and go back down at A. Come up at B and pull the loop gently into place. Go down at C to anchor the loop.

2 Come up at D and slide the ribbon under the base of the Lazy Daisy. Go down at E.

3 Make a Colonial Knot (page 63) at the base of the Lazy Daisy. Add a Stem Stitch (page 164) for the stem and long Japanese Ribbon Stitches (page 106) for leaves.

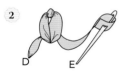

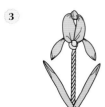

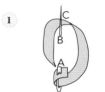

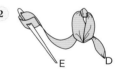

LEFT- AND RIGHT-HANDED

Use 4mm ribbon for small roses or 7mm ribbon for medium roses.

1 Stitch 3 Japanese Ribbon Stitches (page 106) close together.

2 Fill in with thread French Knots (page 94). These will show toward the top and will act as padding for the overlapping stitches.

3 Add 3 Japanese Ribbon Stitches in front, keeping them very loose. Use the needle to slide under each stitch and gently pull to give it more fullness.

4 Add 2 longer Japanese Ribbon Stitches. Roses can be made much larger and looser by adding more petals and varying shades.

1

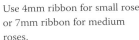

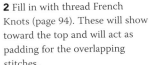

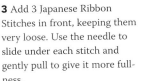

2

3

4

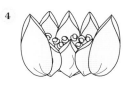

105

Japanese Ribbon Stitch

1 Come up at A, make sure the ribbon lies flat on the fabric, and pierce the center of the ribbon at B.

2 Gently pull through to the back. The ribbon edges will curl at the tip. (The whole effect will be lost if the ribbon is pulled too tight.)

Variation

Japanese Wire Ribbon Bud

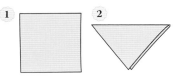

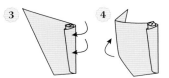

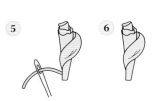

1 Use a wide, wire-edged ombre ribbon. Cut a piece the exact length of the ribbon width to form a square.

2 Fold the piece into a triangle, with the fold on top.

3 Fold one wing tightly into the center.

4 Fold the other wing backward and down, keeping it rather loose, to form a bud or lily shape.

5–6 Using a needle and a strong thread, pierce the bottom of the bud and wrap tightly. Make a knot. Trim off the excess ribbon and sew the bud into place.

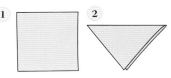

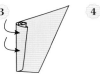

Joyce Flower Fargo Flower (Joyce Valley)

1 Use about 12″ of 4mm silk ribbon and a chenille needle. Come up at A and hold the ribbon in your free hand.

2 With the tip of the needle held very close to point A, take 3 to 5 long Running Stitches through the ribbon.

3 Gently pull the needle to gather the ribbon.

4–5 Go back down (as close to A as possible but not into it). Pull the ribbon through and gently pull into place.

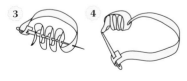

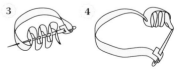

Judith's Curled Leaf

1 Come up at A. Slide the needle under the ribbon to smooth it out. Decide on the length of the stitch, and with the tip of the needle at B, push the ribbon (in the center) into a curl or curve.

2 Pierce through to the fabric below and gently pull the ribbon through. Use your finger or a laying tool to keep the ribbon smooth and even. Do not let the ribbon twist.

3–4 Pull until a small roll appears at the tip of the leaf. Be careful not to pull too tightly or the leaf will disappear into a small, short Japanese Ribbon Stitch (page 106)!

1

2

3

4

1

2

3

4

Judith's Knotted Flowers

LEFT-HANDED

1 Draw a flower outline onto the fabric. Use about 12″ of 4mm silk ribbon and a chenille needle. Come up at A.

2 Make a knot at the desired height (¼″ to ½″). With the needle tip, work the knot into place to tighten. Go down at A.

3–4 Come up again near A, and use the needle as a laying tool to make sure both sides of the knot are even. Repeat the process until the area is filled.

RIGHT-HANDED

Lazy Daisy Stitch

1 Come up at A and form a loop. Go down at B (as close to A as possible, but not into it), then up at C, bringing the needle tip over the thread.

2–3 Go down at D, making a small anchor stitch.

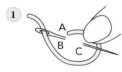

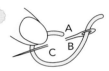

Lazy Daisy Stitch—Bullion Knot

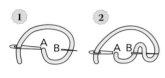

1 Bring the thread up at A. Form a loop. Go down at A and come out at B. Pull the loop snug under the needle.

2 Take the thread going into the needle and wrap the thread around the needle tip.

3 Make 4 or 5 wraps. Pull the wraps snugly.

4–5 Hold the wraps firmly with your thumb and pull the thread through the wraps. Pull the wraps tight. Anchor the stitch. Use the tip of the needle to push the wraps into place.

RIGHT-HANDED

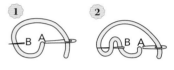

LEFT-HANDED

1 Come up at A and form a loop. Go down at B (as close to A as possible, but not into it) then up at C, bringing the needle tip over the ribbon. Keep the ribbon flat and wrap the ribbon around the needle 2 or 3 times.

2 Hold the twists in place with your thumb and pull the needle through.

3–4 Hold the twists firmly on the fabric and go down at D, anchoring the stitch to the fabric.

RIGHT-HANDED

Lazy Daisy Stitch—Decorative

1 Come up at A and form a loop. Go down at B then up at C, bringing the needle tip over the thread. If using ribbon, keep it flat.

2–3 Go down at D, forming a small anchor stitch at the top of the loop. With another color thread or ribbon, come up again at A then go down just below C.

1

2

3

1

2

3

Lazy Daisy Stitch—Double

1 Come up at A and form a loop. Go back down at A, then come up at B. Make sure the needle lies over the thread; pull through. Go down at C.

2–3 Come up just above A, and form a larger Lazy Daisy on the outside.

Variation

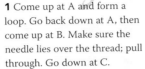

LEFT-HANDED

1

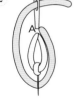

2

3

RIGHT-HANDED

1

2

3

Lazy Daisy Stitch—French Knot

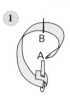

LEFT-HANDED

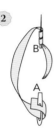

1 Using a 4mm ribbon, come up at A. Make a loop, go back down in A, and up at B. Pull the loop under the needle tip at B.

2 Extend the needle's tip, but not the eye, over and beyond the loop. Raise the needle tip by applying pressure to the eye of the needle. Wrap the ribbon twice around the needle. Holding the wraps, pull the needle and the ribbon firmly through.

3–4 Catch the ribbon loop with the needle as you go back down, as close to B as possible.

Variation

RIGHT-HANDED

Lazy Daisy Stitch—Rose

LEFT- AND RIGHT-HANDED

1 Come up at A and go down at B to make a Japanese Ribbon Stitch (page 106).

2 Come up at A and make a Lazy Daisy Stitch (page 111).

3 Come up at A again and make a larger Lazy Daisy Stitch on the other side.

4 Starting at the bottom center of the petals, make a Straight Stitch to each side. Work a third Straight Stitch in the center.

(1)

(2)

(3)

(4)

Lazy Daisy Stitch—Rosebud

1 Come up at A and form a loop. Go back down at A then come up at B. As you tighten the loop, keep it as flat and smooth as possible. Working the ribbon gently into place, pull the ribbon through B.

2 Pierce the ribbon at the top of the loop and pull into place to secure the stitch, letting this catch stitch remain a bit loose.

3–4 With thread or yarn, make a Fly Stitch (page 88) and a Colonial Knot (page 63) at the base to form the calyx.

Variation

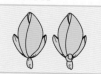

Leaf Ribbon Stitch

1 Mark a line the desired length of the leaf. Come up at A and go down at B, forming a Straight Stitch, then come up at C.

2–4 Go down at D, to the right and even with C (to the left and even with C if left-handed), and up at E, bringing the needle tip over the ribbon. Go down at F, forming a small anchor stitch. Continue with the next stitches, flaring out wider and wider to form a leaf.

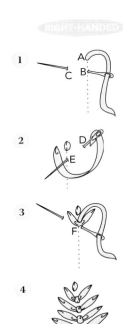

Leaf Stitch

LEFT-HANDED

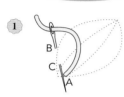

1 Mark the shape to guide the stitches. Come up at A, go down at B, and up at C.

2–3 Work the stitches alternately on either center line to keep the spacing consistent. Continue in this manner, alternating from side to side, until the shape is filled. An outline of Stem (page 164) or Chain Stitches (page 46) is usually worked around the leaf.

RIGHT-HANDED

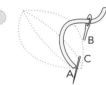

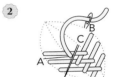

Leaves (Ribbon)

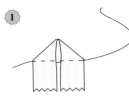

1 Depending on the size of the ribbon, these leaves can be $\frac{1}{8}''$–$2''$ wide. Cut a length of ribbon 3 ribbon widths long. (For example, a $\frac{1}{2}''$-wide ribbon would be cut $1\frac{1}{2}''$ long.) Fold into a prairie point (with raw edges folded down to the base). Baste along the wide edge.

2–3 Pull the thread to gather. Make a knot and leave a short tail for tacking.

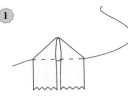

Long and Short Stitch

1 Mark the shape as a guide for the stitches. Come up at A and go down at B, making a Straight Stitch the desired length, then come up at C.

2 Work the first row in alternating long and short Satin Stitches, keeping the outline of the shape even and defined.

3–4 Work the remaining Satin Stitch rows in equal lengths; vary the thread color to add shading. Use this stitch for shading or filling in large areas.

①

②

③

④

①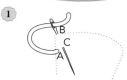

②

③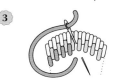

④

Loop Flower

1 Draw a small circle as a guide for the stitches and mark the points of each petal (can be 3, 4, or 5 petals).

2 Come up at A and go down ¹⁄₈″ away at B. Over a round toothpick, adjust the loop to be as long as the radius of the circle. Keep the toothpick in place until you complete the next loop to avoid pulling the previous one out of shape.

3–4 After completing the petals, thread an embroidery needle with floss and add French Knots (page 94) or Pistil Stitches (page 140) to the flower center to anchor the loops.

1

2

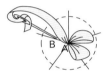

3

4

1

2

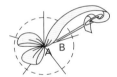

3

4

Loop Flower—Bud

LEFT-HANDED

RIGHT-HANDED

1 Come up at A and go down at B. Gently pull the ribbon to form a loop, not letting the ribbon twist. Use your finger or a laying tool to keep the loop straight. Pull the loop to the desired size.

2–4 Thread a needle with the desired thread. Flatten the ribbon loop, so the loops are even. Bring the thread up through the center of the loop. Make a French Knot (page 94) to anchor. Pull the thread tightly so the 2 sides of the ribbon form a bow.

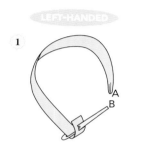

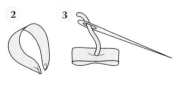

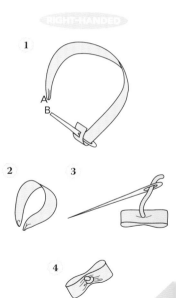

Loop Stitch—Single

1-2 Using 4mm silk ribbon, come up at A and go back down at B. Use your finger or a laying tool to prevent the loop from twisting. Gently pull the loop to the desired length.

Work the loops close together. (Use caution, this stitch is easily pulled out.)

Loop Stitch (Thread)

1 Work this stitch, along 3 parallel lines. Come up at A and go down at B. Come up at C (even with and directly below B), looping the thread under the first stitch and bringing the needle tip over the thread.

2–3 Continue working the next stitch, going down at D and emerging at E.

1

2

3

1

2

3

Magic Chain Band Stitch

LEFT-HANDED

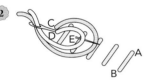

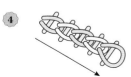

1 Come up at A and go down at B to make a line of Straight Stitches.

2 Thread the needle with 2 contrasting threads. Come up at C, loop only one thread under the needle, go down at D (as close to C as possible, but not into it), and up at E, bringing the needle tip over one of the threads as shown. That thread will appear as a single Chain Stitch and the second thread will disappear behind the fabric.

3–4 Repeat the stitch, working the second thread under the needle. Continue stitching, alternating the first and second threads for the loops.

RIGHT-HANDED

Maidenhair Stitch

1 Come up at A, go down at B, and up at C, bringing the needle tip over the thread.

2–3 Work 3 single feather-stitches on one side, graduating the length of the stitches and aligning them vertically. Work a similar group of stitches on the opposite side.

1

2

3

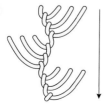

1

2

3

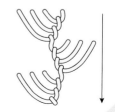

Mokuba Flower

LEFT- AND RIGHT-HANDED

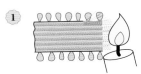

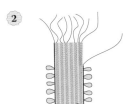

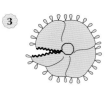

1 Cut a $1\frac{1}{2}$" length of Mokuba picot-edge polyester ombré ribbon. Burn one cut end. It will leave a hard, melted edge.

2 Unravel the widthwise thread on the unburned end to make fringe.

3 Decide if the flower will have a light or dark center. Holding the ribbon loosely, pull the outside vertical thread of the dark or light center side until that side is tightly gathered. Holding the gathered side in place, burn the second raw edge as in Step 1 to melt the threads together and hold the gathered edge in place.

4–5 Let one end overlap the other to form a small, cupped flower. Sew it into place with matching thread. Fill in the center with beads or French Knots (page 94).

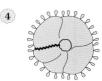

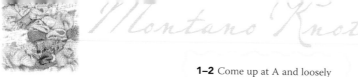

Montano Knot

LEFT-HANDED

1

2

1–2 Come up at A and loosely wrap the thread around the needle (wrap 1 to 6 times depending on the desired size). Insert the needle back into the fabric (as close to A as possible but not into it). Pull through, but do not hold the ribbon off to one side as with other knots. Avoid pulling the stitch too tight; the knot should be loose and flowery.

RIGHT-HANDED

1

2

Needleweaving Bar Stitch

LEFT-HANDED

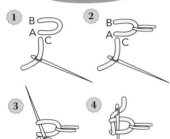

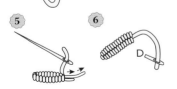

1 Come up at A. Form a loop and go down at B. Decide how wide the bar should be and make the loop that width. Come up just below A at C.

2 Pass a bobby pin, a paper clip, or a thread through the loop to hold the loop off the fabric.

3 Weave *over* the bottom thread and *under* the top thread.

4 Come back *over* the top thread and *under* the bottom. After each pass, push the woven thread snugly down to the previous wraps.

5 Once the loop is completely wrapped, remove the bobby pin, paper clip, or thread.

6–7 Make the bar curve by going into the fabric at D (just a bit shorter than the length of the bar).

RIGHT-HANDED

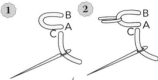

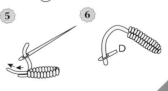

{131}

Net Stitch

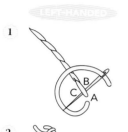

1

2

3

1 Make a row of Stem Stitches (page 164) to act as an anchor for the first row. Using a new thread, come up on the end of the Stem Stitch row at A. Holding down the thread, slide the needle under the first Stem Stitch, forming a loose Buttonhole Stitch (page 36). Make sure the needle lies over the loop.

2 Continue down the row.

3 Repeat this process for each row.

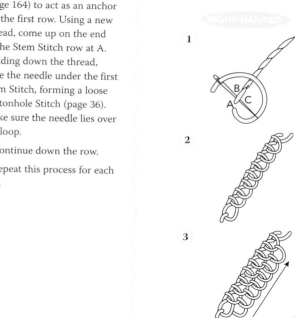

1

2

3

Open Square Stitch

1 Come up at A and go down at B, making a Straight Stitch the desired length; then, up at C.

2 Make a Backstitch at B and emerge at D.

3–5 Continue in this manner. Work in successive rows for borders or as filler.

LEFT-HANDED

1

2

3

4

5

RIGHT-HANDED

1

2

3

4

5

Overcast Stitch

1–3 Mark a line the designated length of the Overcast Stitch. Cut threads to this length and place them on the marked line. Come up at A. Holding the cut threads on the marked line, go down at B and up at C, working small Satin Stitches with the wrapping thread. Keep the wraps close and even. When finished, take the ends of the cut threads to the back and secure.

LEFT-HANDED

1

2
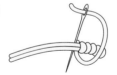

3

RIGHT-HANDED

1

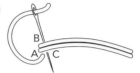

2
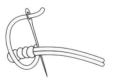

3

Oyster Stitch

1 Come up at A and form a loop. Go back down at B then come up at C, with the needle over the thread. Pull the stitch into place.

2 Slide the needle under the thread, just below A.

3 Pull the thread through and allow the thread to lie on the side of the twisted chain.

4 Go down inside the loop to the right of the twist (to the left if left-handed). Come up at the base, with the needle over the loop.

5 Pull the thread through; the second loop lies around the first loop. Anchor the loop by taking a stitch.

Palestrina Knot

LEFT-HANDED

1 Come up at A, go down at B, then up at C. Slide the needle under the stitch.

2 Loop the thread around the stitch again, bringing the needle tip *over* the thread this time.

3–4 Pull the thread to form a knot, then go down at D, and up at E to continue the next stitch.

RIGHT-HANDED

LEFT-HANDED

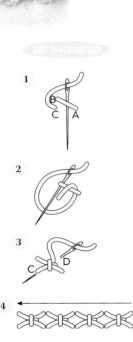

1 Come up at A, go down at B, then up at C, keeping the stitches relatively loose. Slide the needle under the stitch, looping the thread around the stitch.

2-4 Loop the thread around the stitch again, bringing the needle tip over the thread this time. Pull the stitch snugly and go down at D. To make a continuous row, come up again at C (point A of the next stitch).

RIGHT-HANDED

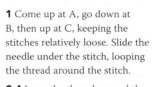

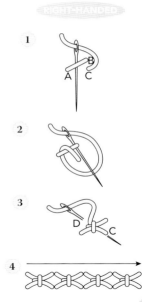

Pansy Stitch

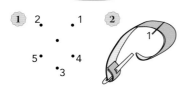

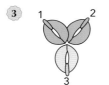

1–2 Mark dots. Select 4 shades of 4mm silk ribbon. Thread a chenille needle with the base shade (on top) and one of the remaining shades. Treat it as a single ribbon. Come up at the center mark and work a loose loop. Make a stitch to secure the loop, making a Lazy Daisy (page 111).

3 Make a second Lazy Daisy (2). Using the base shade and the second shade, work the next petal (3). The second shade goes on top.

4 Using the third and base shade, work the remaining (4 and 5) petals. The third shade goes on top. Work a Colonial Knot (page 63) in the center. Using dark thread, work a Straight Stitch (page 67) in the center of the 3 bottom petals.

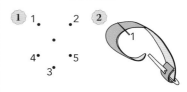

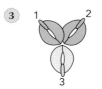

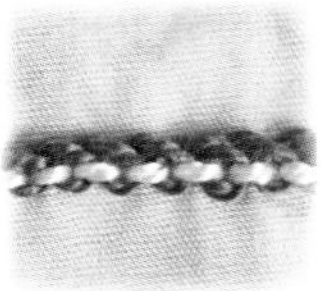

Pekinese Stitch

1 Come up at A, go down at B, and up at C.

2–4 Make a line of Backstitches (page 26). Using a thread of the same or a contrasting color, come up at 1, slide the needle under the previous Backstitch, and loop the thread under the first Backstitch, bringing the needle tip over the thread.

Variation

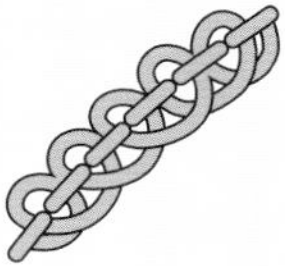

LEFT-HANDED

1
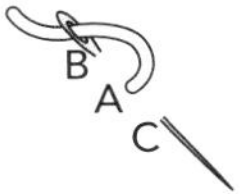

2
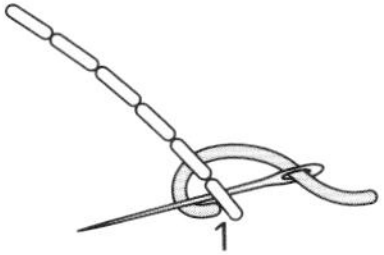

3
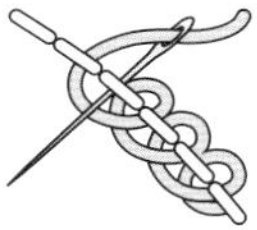

4
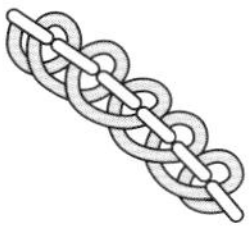

RIGHT-HANDED

1
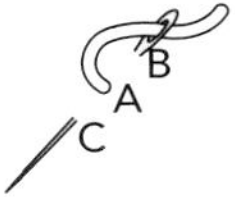

2
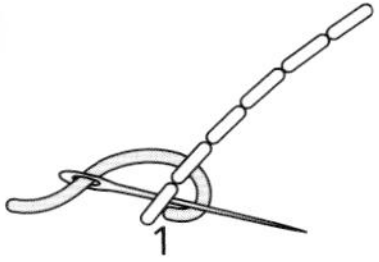

3
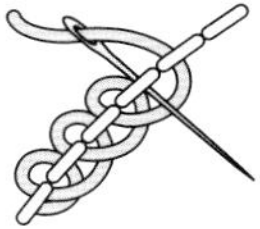

4
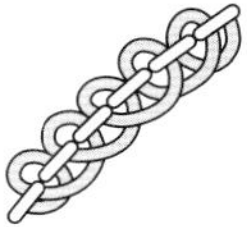

Pistil Stitch

1 Come up at A, allowing a short length of thread, and wrap the working thread twice around the needle to form a French Knot.

2–3 Go down at B (the length of the short thread plus the French Knot), holding the knot in place until the needle is completely through the fabric.

Plume Stitch

1 Come up at A and go down ⅛″ away at B to make a loop; control it with a round toothpick.

2–3 Hold the loop in place and come up at C, piercing both the fabric and the previous ribbon loop. Form another loop. Continue working downward until the plume is finished.

1

2

3

1

2

3

Portuguese Knotted Stem

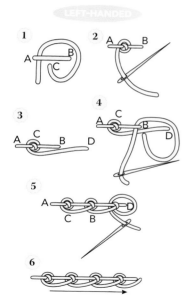

1 Come up at A and go down at B. Come up at C, below the bar. Wrap the thread up and over the bar. Come down under the bar on the side of C. Pull gently into place.

2 Wrap around a second time, bringing the needle under the bar, between the knot and A. Pull gently into place.

3 Insert the needle at D.

4 Come back up at B, below the bar, for the second knot.

5–6 Repeat the same process to finish the desired length.

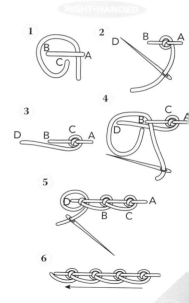

142

Raised Ribbon Stitch

LEFT-HANDED

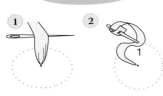

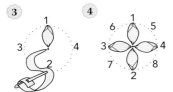

1 Draw a circle the desired size of the flower, with a dot in the center. Come up with the ribbon, just above the center dot. Use the needle to flatten the ribbon.

2 Gently raise the ribbon to form a curve, and pierce the ribbon at the drawn-circle line (in the center of the ribbon).

3 Carefully pull the ribbon through, until the end starts to curl and pops through. Come up directly below the dot in the center, and create the second petal.

4 Add petals 3 and 4 to make a cross. Add petals 5, 6, 7, and 8 to make a full flower.

5 Add French Knots (page 94) to the center.

RIGHT-HANDED

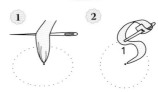

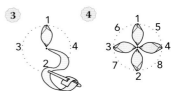

Raised Straight Stitch

LEFT-HANDED

1 Mark the outer circle shape with dots. Mark a second smaller circle in the center. Divide the circle into quarters as shown. Come up on the center circle and go down on the outer circle.

2 Work the quarter circle with Straight Stitches.

3–4 Complete the circle. Fill the center with French Knots (page 94). Raise the Straight Stitches by running the needle under the stitches, gently pushing them up.

RIGHT-HANDED

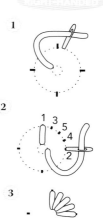

Rambler Rose

LEFT-HANDED

1 Work a small cluster of French Knots (page 94) for the center. Come up at A, go down at B, then up at C.

2–3 Work 2 or 3 rounds of loose Stem Stitches (page 164) around the knot. Make the Stem Stitches longer with each round.

RIGHT-HANDED

1

2

3

1

2

3

Ribbon Split Stitch

1 Come up at A and go down at B. Use the needle to keep the ribbon flat.

2 Come up in the center of the Straight Stitch at C, flatten the ribbon with the needle, and go back down at D.

3 Continue stitching for the desired length.

Ribbon Stitch Pansy

LEFT-HANDED

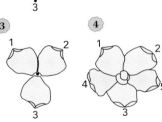

1 Mark dots as shown.

2 Come up just beyond the center dot. Slide the needle under the ribbon to flatten and gently lift it. Pierce the ribbon in the center at the marked dot (1). Pull the ribbon through until it curls making a Japanese Ribbon Stitch, page 106.

3 Work the next petal (2) until it is snug against the first. Change the color of ribbon and work the bottom petal (3) in the same way. Use your needle to spread the ribbon.

4–5 Using a third shade of ribbon, make the final two stitches. Fill the center with a loose Colonial Knot (page 63). Using a dark thread, put in three fan-shaped Straight Stitches on each of the three bottom petals.

RIGHT-HANDED

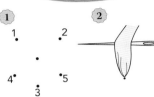

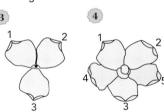

Rosette Bud

1–2 While keeping the ribbon flat, come up at A and go down at B, making a small Straight Stitch. Come up at C and go down at D creating a padded Straight Stitch; do not pull the ribbon tight.

3–4 Angle a second padded stitch to one side, covering the base of the first. Angle a third, padded stitch to the other side of the first stitch, covering the base of the second.

LEFT-HANDED

1

2

3

4

RIGHT-HANDED

1

2

3

4

Rosette Stitch

1 Come up at A and make a loop, go down at B, then up at C, leaving the needle in the fabric.

2 Pull the working thread up and carefully wrap it around the needle 3 or 4 times. Try to keep the threads flat and side by side.

3–4 Pull the needle through slowly and go down at D, tacking the rosette at both ends.

Running Stitch

1–2 Come up at A, go down at B, then up at C, continue making small, even stitches that are the same length as the spaces between them.

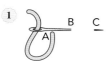

① B C

A

②

① C B

A

②

1 Come up at A and go down at B, working a line of Running Stitches (page 150).

2–3 Use a thread of the same or a contrasting color and come up at 1, sliding the needle under the Running Stitches at even intervals.

Variation

For a laced stitch use a contrasting thread and come up at 1, sliding the needle under the Running Stitches while working above and below them.

1

2

3

Ruth's Rosette (Ruth Stonely)

LEFT-HANDED

1 Take a length of 4mm silk ribbon. Using a metallic, smooth thread on a fine needle, anchor stitch an end of the ribbon firmly into the edge of the fabric. On the back of the fabric, come up ¼" beyond the anchor stitches. (Keep a ⅛" to ¼" space between each rosette.) Hold the ribbon.

2–4 Take 4 Running Stitches (page 150), so there are 4 "bumps" on the needle. End the needle under the ribbon. Pull the needle and thread through and go back down at A to gather the ribbon.

5–6 Make a knot on the back to hold the flower in place. Hold the remaining ribbon flat and come up in the middle, ¼" away from the flower. Repeat to make the next flower.

RIGHT-HANDED

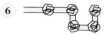

Satin Stitch

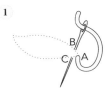

1 Mark the shape as a guide for the stitches. Come up at A and go down at B, making a Straight Stitch the desired length; then come up at C.

2–3 Continue working Straight Stitches close together, keeping the edge of the design even and defined. These stitches can be worked in single layers, or double layers to create a thick, smooth blanket of stitching.

153

Scroll Stitch

1–3 Come up at A. Loop the working thread to the right (to the left if left-handed) and hold it in place with your thumb. Go down at B and emerge at C, making a small, slanted stitch in the center of the loop. Tighten the loop around the needle and pull the needle through. Continue, to make a line of stitches.

1

1

2

2

3

3

Seed Stitch

1–2 Come up at A and go down at B. Repeat for a second stitch, working the thread in the same holes, side by side.

Variation

Surround the Seed Stitches with an outline of Backstitches (page 26) if you're creating leaves.

1

B A

2

1

A B

2

Sheaf Stitch

LEFT-HANDED

1 Come up at A and go down at B. Work 2 more evenly spaced Straight Stitches of equal length.

2 Come up at the center of the Straight Stitches and loop the thread around the stitches.

3 Pull the loop taut and go back down at the center, forming a catch stitch. For variety, change the length of the stitches, or the number of loops, or move the catch stitch up or down the row of stitches.

RIGHT-HANDED

Side Ribbon Stitch

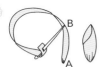

1 Come up at A, using 4mm silk ribbon (or wider). Slip the needle under the ribbon while holding the ribbon in place. Slide the needle down under the ribbon to flatten it. Decide on the length of the stitch and which way the tip will curve.

2 If the ribbon is pierced on the left side (B), the right side will curl in.

3 If pierced on the right side (B), the left side will curl in.

4 Continue making stitches to create a flower.

Snail Trail Stitch

1–3 Work this stitch along a designated line. Come up at A, make a loop, and hold the thread with your thumb. Go down at B, then up at C, bringing the needle tip over the thread. Vary the stitch by altering the stitch spacing and the slant of the needle.

LEFT-HANDED

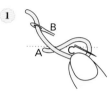

RIGHT-HANDED

Spider Web—Backstitch

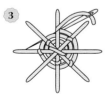

1 Using a tapestry needle, stitch the spokes as shown (up at A, down at B, up at C, down at D, and so on), pulling each spoke firmly into place.

2 Make a small stitch in the center to hold down all the spokes.

3 Come up to the top in the center. Slide the needle under one spoke.

4 Continue working, easing back over 1 spoke and advancing under 2. Continue until the spokes are filled; wrap the thread back around the final spoke.

Variations

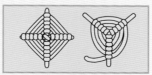

Spider Web—Rose

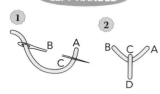

1 With perle cotton or floss, come up at A, go down at B even with and to the right of A (to the left of A is left-handed), then up at C, bringing the needle tip over the thread.

2 Gently draw the thread through the fabric. Go down at D, forming a catch stitch.

3 Add a stitch of equal length on each side, forming 5 spokes. Come up in the center of the spokes with ribbon.

4–5 Working around the center, weave the ribbon over and under the spokes. Keep the ribbon loose and let it twist as you work.

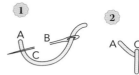

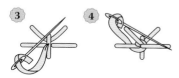

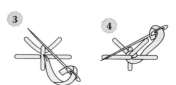

Split Stitch

1–2 Use a heavier thread (that you can split) for this stitch. Come up at A, make a small Backstitch to B, then up at C, piercing the working thread in the middle.

1

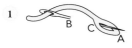

2

1

2

Stab Stitch

1–2 Come up at A and slide the needle under the ribbon to smooth it; go down at B. Ensure that the ribbon lies flat and is not twisted.

Variation

1

1
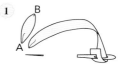

2

2

Star Filling Stitch

1 Come up at A and go down at B. Come up at C, go down at D, then up at E, crossing the stitch with an equally sized horizontal stitch.

2–3 Work slightly smaller diagonal stitches: E to F and G to H. Finish with a tiny center cross.

1

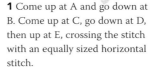

1

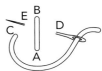

2

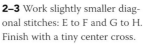

2

3

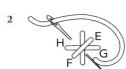

3

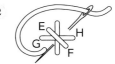

$\mathcal{S}tem$ Stitch

Note: For a straight line of Stem Stitches, the thread length will always be above the line (away from you). For a curved line of Stem Stitches, the thread length will be outside the curved line and the needle will always come up inside the curve (C).

1–3 Come up at A and down at B in a short slanting stitch. Come up at C (the midpoint of A and B). Repeat, keeping the stitches small and uniform.

①

②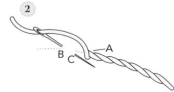

③

①

②

③

$\mathcal{S}tem$ Stitch—Portuguese

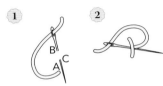

1 Come up at A, go down at B, then up at C (the midpoint of the A/B stitch).

2–3 Pull the thread through and slide the needle under the stitch. Repeat, making 2 loops around the stitch.

4–6 Continue with the next stitch, always working beside the previous stitch.

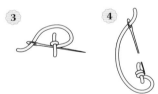

Stem Stitch—Whipped

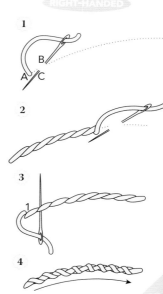

Note: For a straight line of Stem Stitches, the thread length will always be above the line (away from you). For a curved line of Stem Stitches, the thread length will be outside the curved line and the needle will always come up inside the curve (C).

1–2 Come up at A and down at B in a short slanting stitch. Come up at C (the midpoint of A and B). Repeat, the keeping stitches small and uniform.

3–4 Using matching or contrasting thread, come up at 1 and slide the needle under the stem stitches, working the Whip Stitches at even intervals without catching the fabric.

LEFT-HANDED

1

2

3

4

RIGHT-HANDED

1

2

3

4

Straight Stitch

1–2 Come up at A and go down at B, pulling the thread firmly into place. Straight Stitches can be worked evenly or irregularly, varying in length and direction. However, if you make them too loose or too long, they could snag.

①

②

①

②

$\mathcal{S}traight$ Stitch—Bud

LEFT-HANDED

1–2 While keeping the ribbon flat, come up at A and go down at B. Come up at C and go down at D, creating a padded Straight Stitch; do not pull the ribbon tight.

3 Using floss or 2mm ribbon, form the leaves and stem with a Fly Stitch (page 88).

RIGHT-HANDED

1

1

2

2

3

3

Straight Stitch—Rose

1 Come up at A, go down at B, come up at C, go down at D, come up at E, then go down at F.

2–3 Circle the center with 6 Backstitches (page 26). Overlap the joining petal points of the first round with a second round of Backstitches.

1

2

3

1

2

3

String of Pearls Stitch

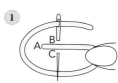

1 Come up at A. Hold the thread in a horizontal line with the left hand (the right hand if left-handed). Hold the needle perpendicular to the thread and take a small stitch down at B, up at C. The tip at the needle lies over the thread; pull firmly into place.

2 Take the thread up under the bar to the right of the knot. Lay the thread in a small circle, surrounding the knot.

3–4 Go down just below the bar at D, close to the knot. Come up next to the knot at E; pull taut. Continue to the desired length of the stitch.

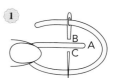

Tube Rose

LEFT-HANDED

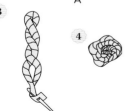

1 Use 14″ of 4mm ribbon and a chenille needle. Come up at A. Hold the needle and ribbon perpendicular to the fabric. Twist the ribbon into a tight tube.

2 Hold the tube securely in the center with your free hand. Fold it in half. Insert the needle near A until only the eye is above the fabric.

3–4 Let go of the ribbon, allowing the 2 halves to twist around each other to form one large tube. Gently pull down and continue pulling until the rose is the desired size. Secure the rose with tiny stitches in the center using fine, matching thread.

RIGHT-HANDED

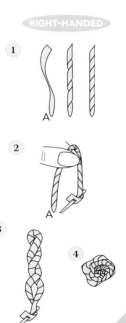

Tulip Stitch

1 Come up at A to form a loop, go down at B, then up at C, bringing the needle tip over the thread.

2 Take a small stitch at D to anchor the bottom of the loop, then come up at E.

3–5 Slide the needle under the anchor stitch and go down at F.

Turkey Work Stitch

LEFT-HANDED

1 Go down at A and leave a ½" tail. Holding the tail under your thumb, come up at B, and go down again at A.

2–3 Come up again at B and trim the second thread tail to match the first. To make a continuous row of uncut stitches, slide a pencil under each loop while stitching to keep the loops uniform.

RIGHT-HANDED

173

Twisted Loop Stitch

1 Come up at A, twist the loop once, and go down at B.

2–4 Hold the loop in place and come up at C, piercing both the fabric and the ribbon loop. To avoid pulling the loops out of shape, use a needle or round toothpick to hold each loop until you come up for the next loop.

LEFT-HANDED

RIGHT-HANDED

Twisted Ribbon Stitch

LEFT-HANDED

1

2

3

1 Come up at A. Decide on the length of the stitch. Twist the ribbon to the desired tightness.

2 Keeping the tension to hold the twists, go down and pull through.

3 Nudge the twisted ribbon into place.

Variations

RIGHT-HANDED

1

2

3

Van Dyke Stitch

1 Work this stitch between 2 parallel lines. Come up at A, go down at B, and come up at C. Go down at D and up at E.

2–3 Slide the needle under the crossed threads and gently pull the loop into place. The V formed at the top of the stitch should flare.

1

2

3

1

2

3

Wheat Ear Stitch

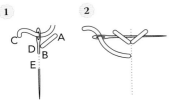

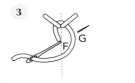

1 Mark a line the desired length of the stitch. Come up at A and go down at B, slanting your stitch, then up at C, even with and to the right of A (to the left of A if left-handed). Go down again at D (as close to B as possible but not into it) and up at E.

2 Slide the needle under the slanted stitches to form a loop.

3-4 Go down again at F (as close to E as possible but not into it), and up at G, bringing the thread over the needle. Continue with the next stitch.

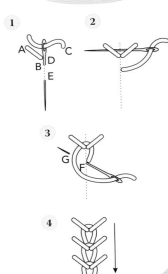

Wheat Ear Stitch—Detached

LEFT-HANDED

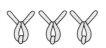

1 Come up at A. Go down at B and back up at C. Keep the needle over the looped thread. Pull down and hold the thread with your free hand.

2–3 Make a second loop. Go down at C and up at D. Anchor with a small stitch.

RIGHT-HANDED

Whip Stitch—Single and Curved

①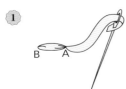

②

③

1 While keeping the ribbon flat, come up at A and go down at B, making a Straight Stitch the desired length. Bring the needle up again at A.

2–3 Depending on the desired effect, wrap the Straight Stitch 2 or 3 times, keeping the ribbon flat. Anchor the stitch by passing the needle to the back.

Variation

Wrap the stitch by first working toward B and then working toward A to crowd the stitch so it will curve.

①

②

③

Wool Rose

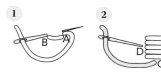

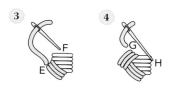

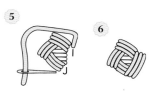

1 Using wool thread, come up at A and down at B. Bring the needle up a few threads above A. Pull the thread through to make the first stitch. Make a total of 5 stitches.

2 With another shade of wool thread, come up at C and down at D. Make a total of 3 stitches.

3 Come up at E and go down on top at F. Make a total of 3 stitches.

4 Come up at G (overlapping F) and go down at H. Make a total of 3 stitches.

5–6 Bring the wool thread up at I (overlapping H) and go down at J (overlapping C). Make a total of 3 stitches to form the fourth petal.

Wool Rosebud

1 Using wool thread, come up at A and down at B.

2 Alternating from side to side, make 4 more flat stitches.

3 With another shade of wool thread, come up left of the base center and take the wool thread to about two-thirds up on the right side. Work 2 more stitches to complete the first petal.

4 With a third shade, come up to the right of the base, overlapping the first petal. Take the thread up two-thirds of the bud. Work 3 stitches to complete the bud.

5 Change to green thread. Make 2 short Straight Stitches (page 167) at the base. Work the stem using a Stem Stitch (page 164) or a Stem Stitch—Whipped (page 166).

Woven Picot Stitch

LEFT-HANDED

1 Using a tapestry needle, work a pyramid of 3 Straight Stitches the desired length of the petal. Make a secure knot at the back to secure the anchor stitches.

2–3 Come up at F. Weave under and over until you come to the tip. Go to the back and make a secure knot.

Variation

RIGHT-HANDED

Combination Stitches

Pyramid Buttonhole + French Knot + Lazy Daisy + Straight Stitch

Curved Buttonhole + Lazy Daisy + French Knot

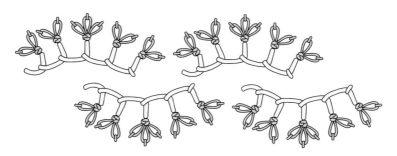

Curved Buttonhole + Colonial Knot + Lazy Daisy

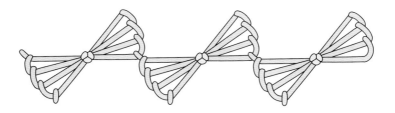

Triangle Buttonhole + Colonial Knot

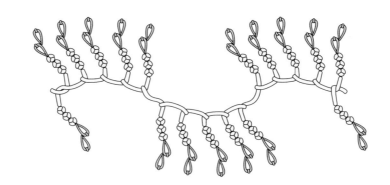

Curved Buttonhole + Colonial Knot + Lazy Daisy

Chain Stitch + Colonial Knot + Lazy Daisy

Chain Stitch + French Knot

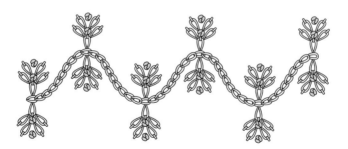

Chain Stitch + French Knot + Lazy Daisy

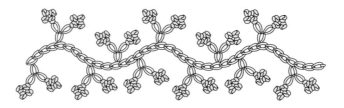

Chain Stitch + French Knot

Chain Stitch + Straight Stitch + French Knot

Cretan Stitch + Lazy Daisy + French Knot

Slanted Cretan Stitch + Straight Stitch + Colonial Knot + Lazy Daisy

Lazy Daisy + Colonial Knot + Stem Stitch

Lazy Daisy with long catch stitch + French Knot + Straight Stitch

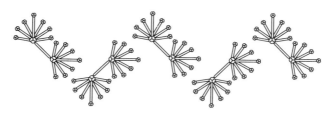

Pistil Stitch + Colonial Knot + Straight Stitch

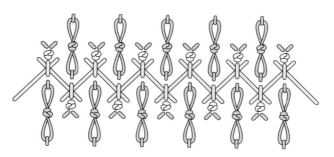

Herringbone + Straight Stitch + Lazy Daisy + French Knot

Long & Medium Lazy Daisy + Colonial Knot

Long & Short Lazy Daisy + Stem Stitch + Pistil Stitch + French Knot

Lazy Daisy + French Knot

Straight Stitch + Lazy Daisy + Colonial Knot